BONE SHOP OF THE HEART

Eugene Mahon is a Training and Supervising psychoanalyst on the faculty of Columbia University Psychoanalytic Center for Training and Research in New York City. He has written poetry since his childhood days in the West of Ireland. He has published three books, *A Psychoanalytic Odyssey: Painted Guinea Pigs, Dreams and Other Realities* Karnac 2014; *Rensal The Redbit: A Psychoanalytic Fairytale* Karnac 2015; *All Serious Daring.* Deluge Books 2013 as well as numerous articles in all the major Psychoanalytic Journals on a great diversity of topics (Dreams, Memory, Repression, Parapraxes, the Golden Section, Play, Mourning, The Oedipus Complex, Insight, Working Through, as well as applied analytic articles on Sophocles, Shakespeare, Coleridge, Wilde). He has written plays (*Yesterday's Silence: A Beckett-Bion dialogue* ; *Anna And Sigmund at The Rue Royale; In The Company Of Ghosts; How Sweet The Moonlight; A Freud-Vitruvius Dialogue; The Death of Hamnet or Hamnet's Last Act.*) He practices Child and Adult Psychoanalysis in New York City.

BONE SHOP
OF THE HEART

EUGENE MAHON

IPBOOKS.net
International Psychoanalytic Books

Copyright © 2017 Eugene Mahon

International Psychoanalytic Books (IPBooks),
30-27 33rd Street, Astoria, NY 11102
Online at: www.IPBooks.net

All rights reserved. This book may not be reproduced, transmitted, or stored in whole or in part by any means, including graphic, electronic, or mechanical without the express permission of the publisher except in the case of brief quotations embodied in critical articles and reviews.

Some of these poems were originally published in *Between Hours: A Collection of Poems by Psychoanalysts*, edited by Salman Akhtar (published by Karnac Books in 2012). I am grateful that Karnac has granted me permission to include them in this new volume.

Book design by Maureen Cutajar

ISBN: 978-0-9980833-4-6

For Delia, of course

ACKNOWLEDGEMENTS

I want to thank those who encouraged my poetry throughout the years. First my wife, muse and extraordinary friend, Delia Battin. The poems that were not written about her directly, certainly have her spirit and imprint on them and in them in profound ways. I want to thank other family members for not only inspiring many of the poems but supporting them as well. Eugene Ross, Lynn, Patrick and Lewis Mahon, John and Ryan Mahon, Emer, Robert , Katrina, Eve and Dillon Svoboda, James, Margaret, Dominic, Rosalind Mahon of London, Paul, Sean, Jason Mahon of Illinois, Dr. Maeve and Patrick Ferriter of Ireland, Magda and Len Brown, Sandra and Mark, Loic and Maelle Brown of London, Olivia, Geoff and Sam Brown of Meilhan Sur Garonne, France.

Then there are friends and colleagues who have always supported a fledgling poet. Their imprint is also palpable in the texture of the poems in subtle, mysterious and inspirational ways. I list them without any sense of order:

Shelly Bach, Phyllis Beren, Lynne Rubin, Mirella and Charles Affron, Clara Genetos, Lydia Katzenbach, Mara Schwartz, Helen and Dick Halverson, Olivia Motch, Laura and Bill Hudson, Alberto Schon of Padua, Italy (who has also translated some of these poems into Italian), Salman Akhtar, Abby Silvan Adams, Mark Silvan, Elizabeth Rich, Joel Markowitz, Gaby and Jesse Hauser, Arnie Richards, Arlene Richards, Carolyn and Steven Ellman, Katherine and Ken Snelson, Merrill and Laurence Cooper, Christianne and Francis Baudry, Charles Winkelstein, Cecily and Steve Firestein, Warren Poland, Robert Michels, Fred Wiener, James Egan, Carol Bandini, Robert Mammarella, Gordon Lish, Phiip Ginsburg, Rachel Ginsburg., Lucio Amadio, Frieda Arkin, Rod Tweedy, Michael Kildea. I want to especially thank David Hurst, artist, psychoanalyst, friend for his most evocative painting "Insight Outlook" which illuminates the book's cover with its haunting, poetic beauty.

PREFACE

One can easily argue that the best training for practicing psychoanalysis is not training in psychiatry or social work or clinical psychology, but rather training in the art of poetry.

For poetry is about bringing alive and making sense out of an often senseless and inanimate world, about infusing a reason for living into a world that is forever collapsing into violence, meaninglessness and despair.

A good-enough poet puts together out of snippets of rag and bone a larger, holistic picture of the human condition, and while this picture may not necessarily be cheery or uplifting, it gives the listener a different perspective, a moment of renewed faith in the human animal and, sometimes, a desire to understand and to go on living.

Some of the ways poetry does this are very similar to what we do in psychoanalysis. Poetry attempts to take disordered fragments of experience and allow them to order themselves into some meaningful whole, much as psychoanalysts do with memories or unformulated experience. Poetry often calls up chaos, and by allowing chaos to exist it witnesses the process of its embodiment into meaningful structures, much as we hold psychotic experiences until they can structure themselves. Good-enough poetry does this unselfconsciously, much as the good-enough analyst also works not from a theory or manual but from the heart.

Eugene Mahon is both a psychiatrist and a poet, so he is as well trained to be a psychoanalyst as one can hope for in this disorderly world. And because he is not only a poet but also a writer of sonnets, he is totally engaged in the process of transmuting concrete, beta and unformulated experience into one of the most complexly evolved and highly symbolic forms we know. His success at these transformations seems at times magical, comparable to what we know in analysis as moments of insight or of transformative experience.

Mahon is a doctor who has thought long and hard about his relationship with his patients, with the therapeutic process and with the world into which we have all been thrown. Like Gogol, Mahon

> *leads us naked through the night*
> *The dark the only overcoat in sight.*

But he never abandons us there, for he knows that

> *My weeping face was hers*
> *Her bleeding face was mine.*

This recognition and acceptance of darkness and suffering gives special weight to love as it emerges in these poems, not as a coat of pigment on the human condition but as the product of an ongoing struggle, painful and joyous, to arrive at a moment of grace.

Mahon writes about Isaac Rosenberg's experience in the trenches during the Great War:

> *In no mans' land rat's flesh and human's blended:*
> *What touched you was the love a rat extended.*
> But he also writes:
> *We are more than flesh and blood in motion:*
> *We are scattered stars, we are the ocean.*

And:

> *Love is my shiver at the touch of you,*
> *My ruin at the loss of you,*
> *My rise from ashes*
> *On return of you.*
> *Love is your light*
> *In dark of me,*
> *Your fire in cave of me,*
> *Your star in night of me,*
> *Your dream in dawn of me.*

Life and death, love and hate, childhood, loss and dreaming are the bones of this poetry. It is with immense pleasure that I have read these poems, been rocked and tossed in their rhythms and learned to see better from them. I commend them to anyone who wants to nourish the wondering child living within.

—Sheldon Bach

CONTENTS

1. ON BEING BORN. 1
2. SIX MONTHS A'GROWIN' 3
3. AFTERBIRTH IS ALL WE ARE. 4
4. AMARCORD. 5
5. BOX OF DARKNESS. 10
6. ISLAND. 11
7. FATHER 13
8. IRELAND: A SONNET 15
9. FATHERS AND SONS. 16
10. HOME. 18
11. SEVERED UNION 1942. 19
12. CLOAK AND DAGGER. 20
13. CLOCKWORK. 21
14. MILANO MARITTIMA 22
15. 1942. 24
16. DIALOGUE. 26
17. GIFTS 28
18. LOSERS WEEPERS 30
19. LOVE 31
20. GEARS OF LOVE. 32
21. THE DAY THEY BOTH SAID YES. 34
22. TWILIGHT. 37
23. FOR ISAAC ROSENBERG 38
24. BECKETT 39
25. IN THE DARK. 40
26. CHAGALL 42
27. DREAM 43
28. GOGOL'S OVERCOAT 44
29. A TOUCH OF LOVE. 45
30. ELLIS ISLAND 46

31.	FILIPPO LIPPI	47
32.	FREUD 1939	48
33.	SUICIDE	49
34.	FUGUE IN FIVE VOICES	50
35.	FIRENZE	53
36.	SONNET: CHARON'S TEARS	54
37.	GLENN GOULD'S HUMMING	55
38.	ICARUS	56
39.	GOLDA (1898-1978)	57
40.	HOLOCAUST MEMORIAL DAY	59
41.	JOSEPH OF NAZARETH	60
42.	JUDAS IN PARADISE	62
43.	AT DEATH'S DOOR	63
44.	MARCUS AURELIUS	64
45.	ON LEARNING ROBERT FROST'S "BIRCHES" BY HEART	66
46.	NIGHT PRAYER	67
47.	POETRY	68
48.	PASTORALE	70
49.	ODE TO A NEW YEAR	71

50.	SEDER.	72
51.	SEPTEMBER	74
52.	SNOW	75
53.	SONNET FOR ARNIE RICHARDS	76
54.	DIALOGUE	77
55.	SONNET FOR A NEW YEAR	78
56.	SWEENEY ASTRAY	79
57.	THE GRAVITY OF LOVE	80
58.	TITHONUS' LAMENT	81
59.	A PAINTED GUINEA PIG	82
60.	"TOUCH ME. REMIND ME WHO I AM"	84
61.	WINDMILL'S SONG	85
62.	VINCENT'S SONG	86
63.	PRAGUE	88
64.	THE PAST	90
65.	RESOLUTIONS	92
66.	PUTTING IN THE SPRING	94
67.	TO A CHILD AT THE END OF ANALYSIS	96

ON BEING BORN

There are no words
For first breath
But when wind
Rushed in
I was riding on air
Like an eagle.
Let me tell you
For nine months
I knew only the ocean
Inside her,
The sweep of her blood
All around me
My only earth and sky,
Her heart beat
My only compass.
Suddenly
Upside down
Inside out
Light grabbed me
As sun threw open
The doors of vision
And ran through
Every room of my house.
But let me tell you
It was the feel
Of her flesh
And his flesh
After my long voyage
That made me human,
As their singing in my ears

ON BEING BORN

Made blood dance
For the first time.
Where do I go from here?
I will bleed
Into my after birth
Day after day
The way a trumpet
Bleeds into its song.

SIX MONTHS A'GROWIN'

Christopher at six months
Lying on his back,
Arms pincering air,
Eyes pincering light,
Searching like juggler
For balls not yet
Created.
Those eyes!
Those busy hands
Create, find, lose
And find again
The juggler's art,
The flick of the wrist,
Reality riding on every
Twist and turn
Of the balls in the air.
Ah, Christopher
In a month you'll know
Your mother so well
You'll scream at strangers.

AFTERBIRTH IS ALL WE ARE

For Shelly Bach

After the first journey out of womb
Through birth canal and first wind-greeting scream,
All other journeys, bearing the stamp of it, assume
A memory of the first, like birth-marked dream.
Did Otto Rank make too much out of it, as if
Birth were trauma, a mark on Cain, before
He slew his brother? Perhaps. Theory's a cliff,
Easy to fall from, facts easy to ignore.
Still, all are born and make the journey out,
Womb-launched, MacDuffs excepted, all life ahead
Like dream you never waken from without
Startling visions, fires of insight in your head.
The cord that tied you to your mother tossed
The heart creates anew all that it lost.

AMARCORD

He remembered the Fair days in Ireland,
The spitting on hands
As bargains were struck,
The sawdust soaking up the spillage
In public houses
As huge heroic hands lifted
Pints of frothing Guinness
To lips that smacked,
Storeys (or so it seemed)
Above the stares
Of wide-eyed children,
While outside on the teeming streets
Beyond the pubs
Doomed cattle
Jostled their slow march towards slaughter.
September evenings in Galway
He remembered fishing off Nimmo's Pier
Under moonlight
When mackerel shimmered,
And shook the surface of the water
So much with their leaping
It seemed like applause
To wide-awake children
Who flung their hooks and lines
And pulled out fish
Almost in the same motion.
"You could catch them with a worm
And a safety pin."
One boy boasted.
"You could catch them with your bare hands."

AMARCORD

Another said.
"Ah, go on out of that." another said.
"You couldn't catch your grandmother's arse
If it was handed to you on a plate."
Winter nights
He remembered shivering between sheets,
Curled up like foetus
Under a weight of blankets,
The warmth of the body eventually
Reaching the cocoon of linen and wool
As this primitive central heating slowly
Returned some heat
To its shivering center.
Winter mornings were another story.
By then the *central heating*
Was at maximum efficiency
And the first foetal scouts
To test the elements
(Usually a brief protrusion of finger or toe)
Sent back reports so unpromising
That school-phobic schemes of colic
And catatonia went racing
Through every hypochondriacal pore
Of the cool-hardy body.
He remembered confessions
In dark boxes of fear,
Heart in mouth
"Bless me father."
Trembling on tongue,
"Curse you father."

AMARCORD

Unspoken somewhere deep inside him.
He remembered tenebrae in darkened churches,
Good Friday services,
When a thousand monks
Closed their bibles all at once
Under the ghosts of a thousand flickering candles
And made a thunder
To awaken drowsy children
And the dead.
If Christ was not risen by that racket,
Our faith was surely shaken.
He remembered the town-fools:
"Sweet-sixteen"
Was sixty-six if she was a day,
Trudging to mass
In black mini skirts
That showed a phosphorescent
Sliver of her thighs
That leapt like mackerel
Above black stockings,
A caricature of sex
And Christian piety
That children were afraid to laugh at,
Afraid to pity.
"Currant-cake" was another matter.
An angry loner,
You called him "Currant-cake"
And if you ran fast enough
You might escape his lashes.
"Shoots" beloved "Shoots"

AMARCORD

Was special.
Shell-shocked once upon a time
In a war
Older than children's memories,
He could pull imaginary guns
From hidden holsters
Faster than the fastest child
In the wild wests of Galway.
For an instant
The psychotic Flanders of his mind
And the mad playgrounds of childhood
Met in a grip of recognition,
His terrible memory
Brooding over dreams of youth,
Ghosts and war playing
Cat and mouse.
He remembered Stephen Shea,
Professor of Anatomy,
Lifting up a skull like Yorick's
And telling a joke
About the foramen magnum,
That huge hole in the base of the skull
That admits the upwardly mobile
Spinal column
Into the lofty salons of the mind.
"Many's the fine pint went down there."
He'd laugh,
Mimicking the drunkard's accent
Who confused his mouth
With another hole in his head.

AMARCORD

He remembered leaving Ireland
Watching it grow smaller at lift-off
Memory an engine that failed
Never getting off the ground.
He remembered children arriving from afar
Their accents thick with the scent of home.

BOX OF DARKNESS

"Bless me, father, for I have sinned" he said.
"This is your first good confession?"
"Yes, father."
"How have you sinned in thought, word and deed?"
"I cursed my parents."
"How many times have you sinned in this way?"
"I don't remember."
Suddenly a whispered threat:
"It's important to remember the number."
"Four times, father."
The quick lie appeased the darkness:
(Ever since a hatred of numbers.)
The West of Ireland.
Nineteen hundred and forty seven.
Endless twilight in July,
Not enough light in December
To find a fallen shilling with.
Children talking in the ageless dark
Telling sins to artificial night.
Seven years old.
The age of reason
According to Aquinas.
Old enough to spill
Guilt into a box of darkness
And fill up again with light.
Old enough to lie.
Anonymous priest,
Keeper of the keys
Of the kingdom of darkness,
Their lies were lost on you.

ISLAND

"The sky opened."
Was his mother's way
Of saying it rained
In Ireland.
They have words for the weather there.
Here,
We count it and number it.
There,
They know measuring something
Won't make it better or worse.
So they're content
To describe and accept it:
"A soft day, thank God."
They'll say,
As if they've felt it,
Tried it on, and will continue
To wear it for a while.
They extend a weather-worn hand,
Dip it in the atmosphere
And with oracular voice say:
"There's rain on the wind."
As they offer the prediction
Their confidence implies
An intimacy with wind and rain
That makes privilege possible.
An island surrounded by weather
As firmly as by the sea,
Accepts its bondage
With the dumb grace
Of a horse and cart

ISLAND

Tied to each other,
Hoof answering wheel
In a bitter litany of grievance.
An island doesn't count
The links of chain
That bind it.
It is content to wildly sing beneath
The openings and closings of the sky.

FATHER

His shoes,
The heels I mean,
Were all worn
On one side
As if they kept
A perfect record
Of his walking,
The particular inclination
Of his soles
As leather hit concrete.
When he peeled
An apple
The knife lifted
The whole skin
Off the glisten
Of the fruit
In one continuous
Strand
That dropped eventual
To the floor,
A perfect coil
Of memory
That made a child
Feel
He could replace
The shed skin
With one contrary motion
If he were a magician.
He was. He is.
Sixty years later

FATHER

With the speed of thought
He can resole
His father's shoes,
Clothe the apple again
With a glisten of skin
As if the wound of time
Had never put
A knife to him.

IRELAND: A SONNET

Is it a country or a state of mind,
A wind that accents human speech, a voice
In turn that accents wind, both entwined
In mutual give and take? Does a man have a choice
To step out of the elements that wombed him,
The soil, the roots, the muttering Rahoon rain,
The sun that coaxes memory out of limb
And leaf, the mind that soars against the grain?
"To enter in these bonds is to be free"
Donne said: he knew that love fought
Against its very nature foolishly.
Only a thief sells what he never bought.
In Ireland stonewalls lift their lace against the sky
And twilight never lets an evening die.

FATHERS AND SONS

> "We are what we were."
> —James Joyce

Begetting doesn't end it:
Learning from each
Other
We out-seed ourselves;
In time
Who can tell
Who fathered whom?
In the name of the father
The son finds his way;
In the name of the son
The father's shoulders
Handed down
Become the perch
Of future generations,
History
No more
Than a father's word
Remembered,
A son's promise kept.
Begetting doesn't end it:
Learning from each
Other
We are more than
The sum of ourselves:
Together,
Evening after evening,
With solar eyes
We hang

FATHERS AND SONS

The doomed moon
In the night space,
And break the bread
Of dawn
Again and again
On the cliffs of morning
As we rediscover
The wild pulse of ourselves
And the great goat-footed heart
That keeps pace with the sun!

HOME

A young robin,
Ear still cocked
For messages
From that voice
That first fed worms
Into the gaping beak,
Still has not made
The wind her home
And listens, all intent,
Even as she pecks
Green slabs of earth,
With stiff backed curtsies
Like an oriental politician.
How soon the wind
Will feel like nest enough,
And the mother's voice
A send-off,
Not a call
To hurry home.

SEVERED UNION 1942

> "...a short season between two silences..."
> —Virginia Woolf

They always ran together word and fact,
The sky on the roof so calm, the rain on wind
Like horse and rider: always, until the pact
Was broken and knives of war skinned
Rabbit and crushed the magic hat before
The sleight of hand got started, "war" a word
And "Jew" another that shook the house, tore
Rafters down. It never even occurred
To her at six that words could fail, could fall,
That hearts could break like china, that falling down
Like "ashes, ashes" in the song wasn't all
There was to death in country or in town.
Across the fields she ran as fast as death,
Killing her fear with every brazen breath.

CLOAK AND DAGGER

I was a child
When Death first
Pushed a silencer
In my ribs
And slowly squeezed the trigger.
I never heard the click
Or the released finger.
I have searched
Everywhere,
In every fold of silence
For that sound,
Like a child
At the door
Of the room
He locked the monsters in
Before he went to bed
And tried to sleep.
In the end
And finally out of earshot
I will hear it
When sound
No longer reaches me.

CLOCKWORK

When I jiggled
The pendulum,
Got it going again,
Gravity restored
To its restless swinging,
I had an instant fear
That Time reinstated
Would run circles
Round my face
Not forever.

MILANO MARITTIMA

We woke on the sand
An Adriatic sky above us
Stars all fled
Except for the stragglers.
"The ones who never leave
No matter when the party ends"
You said. "The ones
Who never leave the sea
No matter where the tide is"
I said. We laughed
And the dreams came back to us,
Our two childhoods
Spread out like chess
Pieces or marbles
From a game begun
An age ago, never ending
Until all the stars
Are gone, the skies too,
And even the children,
When the elemental bang
Recedes back into
Its initial silence.
In a dream we were holding
Two concentric hoops,
A balancing act,
As if the sky would fall
If we let go.
"Two childhoods intertwined"
You said.
"Only two?" I laughed

MILANO MARITTIMA

Picturing generations
Since Adam or Lucy
Balancing concentric hoops
Like ripples
Reaching way beyond
The milky ways of love.
You put your hand
In mine.
The stars had gone
To tend to other skies
Beyond our night,
Our dreams as intertwined
As flesh can ever be.

1942

Under a field of stars
Out of hatred
A child is running
Holding up the falling of a sky
That staggers and stumbles,
Too much wine of war
Gone to its head,
Her own hair on fire
In dreams that flash like lightning
In the dark inside her.
Nameless she is running
Under an Aryan sky,
Under the Bear and the Hunter
Naming the stars as she runs,
Her mother runs,
And her mother's mother,
All three running inside
Each other,
Holding on and letting go,
Running into the future,
Running out of the past,
Running into the lives of children,
Running into Sabrina,
Patrick and loic and Lewis,
Katrina and Maelle too,
And Eve and Dillon,
Clearing their fields of jackals
And jackboots,
Making it safe to run,
Making a bonfire of hatred,

1942

Warming the hands of fear on it,
Calling fear by its new name:
She calls it courage,
She carries it into their dreams.
When they wake under a field of stars
They feel her running inside them,
Her words running into theirs
As she whispers into the dreamspace:
"Love is the only captivity
Whose bonds can set you free."

DIALOGUE

The night was full of young stars.
Why did I call them young?
Was that where childhood went
While dreams were aging
As we slept?
So many words were trampled
On the way to the poem.
Which way was it anyway?
The unmarked way.
How did you find it?
By losing my comings and goings.
Were you afraid? Yes.
Lost? Yes. Lonely? Yes.
How will you return?
By another way.
Will we be the same?
Absence will have changed us,
A foretaste of death.
How will we live with it?
Call it Time when your heart
Pounding at the wrist
Can go no further and counts on
What it heard before.
How will we recognize ourselves?
We are the ones in daylight
With night streaks in our hair.
We are the whiteness of daylight
Shadowing stars at night.

1942

We are the only mirrors
That question the sun.
We are night-fishers
Who dive for dreams in the dark.

GIFTS

> My bounty is as boundless as the sea; my love as deep.
> The more I give to thee the more I have for both are infinite.
> —William Shakespeare

I would give you the brazen
Look of flowers
Standing their ground
Before the wind.

I would give you
The life of flowers
Living on in words
When blooms are gone.

I would give you
Desire itself
Before memory
Ran off with it.

I would break
The bread of my mouth
Across the wheat
Of yours
Until all the words
Spilled out of me
Never asking for
A syllable back.

GIFTS

My shadow
Without your light
To throw it
Would run back
Lifeless to the sun.

I would climb
All the hills of your body
Until all breath
Is gone from me.

I would give you
The brazen look of flowers
Before there was a word
For the scything wind.

LOSERS WEEPERS

In the space
Between your hand
And the skin
Of my belly
I placed
My hand
In this cave
Of our own making.
You were unaware
Of the pouch
Marsupial
And your pick-pocket
Lover.
I stole all the coins
Of your love
And lost them
With the drop of your hand.

LOVE

> Love like a star
> Once small and far
> Now huge and near.
> —Lee Robinson

I took your hand
Your body too
I couldn't tell your pulse
From mine,
Love left such little
Space between us,
Our bodies
One imprint on sand
Beside a whisper of the sea
Under a thousand
Adriatic stars,
A restless moon,
And a fugitive sun
Only half a world away.

GEARS OF LOVE

We drove around Malpensa
In a rented stick shift
Until we got the hang of it,
The gears of love
I mean
And then made a bee-line
For the Adriatic,
That other Milan,
Marittima,
Like our dreams.
"L'amarrissimo"
d'Annunzio called it,
An Adriatic
So full of salt,
A drowning man
Could never drown,
Or love
Drowning out of its depth
In another
Could learn perhaps
To swim forever.
Not far north of us
Venice,
Adrift in its own reflection
Made a sail of the wind,
An oar of the sky,
As we drifted
Into the salt

GEARS OF LOVE

That got us started,
Kiss on kiss,
Tectonic,
Like the weight of the earth on the sky.

THE DAY THEY BOTH SAID YES

At Orchard Point
The sky pulled faces
All day long:
We didn't care.
So what if they call it Summer here!
After a swim
Without a stitch of clothing,
We dried off,
Shaking ourselves
Like spaniels,
Shivering our way
Back into heat again.
We had read Homer
All morning,
And I said "Let's search
The woods for heroes,"
And you asked
"Is that a kind of flower?"
And we laughed
Until un-petaled,
If we'd been roses.
And I pressed
The flower of my body
On yours,
The leaves applauding
Or was it birds,
Startled
In hidden bushes,
Leaving like gunshot
In a thunder of wings,

THE DAY THEY BOTH SAID YES

And the ensuing silence
More pronounced than ever
With the birds gone,
Memory all that's left of them.
"Did you find them?"
You asked,
And I knew you meant
Heroes or flowers
Or love itself,
Captive
As the sun
That never moves,
Or all the flesh
In orbit
'round it.
And I said yes.
That night
We heard metallic sounds
On the wind,
And I said
"Those birds have metal
In their throat,
A tiny anvil of love
To forge a song with."
And you said
"Some heroes
Are no bigger than my fist"
And you held it up
In the half light
And I swear I could almost see

THE DAY THEY BOTH SAID YES

The sky itself
As light went through
The mirror of your skin.
"Eve was the first hero"
You said:
"She loved knowledge
More than any god
Who'd keep it from her."
"Fear was Adam's god"
I said.
"By not out-spitting
The taste of it
Like metal on his tongue,
He made a hero
Of his quickening pulse,
His blanching flesh,
And left the seed-grown garden
To divinity,
For honest labor in the fields."
You placed
Your hand
In sweat of mine
And you said yes.

TWILIGHT

When night was day
In the half-light
And your flesh was the amber of wine
I kissed 'til your lips were empty
As you poured all your flesh into mine.

The moon was shy
In the shadows
As she lifted her slip
From her head,
Her breasts milk-white
In the half-light
As night shook her limbs in our bed.

FOR ISAAC ROSENBERG

At break of day in the trenches, with a flower
Behind your ear, you were touched by more
Than rat flesh, men falling hour
By hour, like poppies Homer sang of, before
The worldly wars were numbered. Cosmopolitan
Rat, citizen of the world, as Goethe said,
Whose sympathy touched English hands or German,
Walks nationless among the living and the dead.
Un-naturalized, he touches you, makes you rethink
Boundaries flesh set up to keep brother
From brother from brother, as if the rot and stink
Of death distinguished nations, one from the other.
In no mans' land rat's flesh and human's blended:
What touched you was the love a rat extended.

BECKETT

"I wouldn't go as far as that" he said
When asked if Spring renewed his faith in life,
Jumped in his wrist newborn, giddied his head
Like wine, gave him a new slant on the strife
Of existence. "Two shorten a road" he might
Concede, but that's as far as words can lead
When home is out of reach and love's in sight,
And reaching's more than you want, less than you need.
When finite minds invent the infinite
Waiting's worse than reaching unless
The heart that fills and empties calls it
Joy to blood-red life in fierce caress.
We are more than flesh and blood in motion:
We are scattered stars, we are the ocean.

IN THE DARK

Celts
A thousand years ago
Wrote poetry
Lying on their backs
On couches
In darkness.
Sunlight
Could spoil
The inner ferment
Of assonance
And rhyme.
So they spliced
And counted syllables
In pitch-dark,
Stringing
The glistening catch
Of mind-lit nets
Together
Like night fishermen
Under the net
Of the doomed sky
Reaching for flesh
Of unseen fish,
Their deaths,
Like the days and nights
Of their hunters,
Numbered
Like syllables
In lines of verse.

IN THE DARK

They needed dark
To ghost their twilight
Word trysts.
Dead to the world
They pulled their poems
Like dreams from sleep,
Ghosts to outlast
The words that breed.

CHAGALL

He bolted out of the dream
Threw images
On canvas
The flying clock
The people floating above
The houses
The donkey-headed groom
The luminous bride
The startled sky
Like an ill-fitting hat
On a half-cocked world
Fleeing from yet another
War or pogrom
Life the only god he knew
Death the only god that mattered,
The paint still wet
On the canvas.

DREAM

Beside me a shaking,
A dream shivering,
A piece of the night
Cornered inside you
Like a wounded animal.
I reach in:
Your flesh bars the way.
Shut out
I can feel the thunder
Of an ocean
I cannot see or hear.
Only morning
Will bring the halves
Of us together
When words split
The dream in two.

GOGOL'S OVERCOAT

Out from under Gogol's overcoat
The story-tellers file, tipping a hat
To stitch-craft; tailors all, they dote
On words that stitch a tattered magic mat,
Can carry Akaky and all dead souls
From Petersburg to Paradise. The file
Is international: stories fill the holes
In a poor man's shoes, make grouches smile,
Make kings adjust their crowns. At night in bed
A story is a star, a light in a dream's
Window, when all the other lights have fled
And the dark is deeper than it ever seems.
Gogol guides us naked through the night,
The dark the only overcoat in sight.

A TOUCH OF LOVE

> "Touch me. Remind me who I am."
> —Stanley Kunitz

Love is my shiver at the touch of you,
My ruin at the loss of you,
My rise from ashes
On return of you.
Love is your light
In dark of me,
Your fire in cave of me,
Your star in night of me,
Your dream in dawn of me.
You are memory
Of leaves in Springtime
Before my leaves arrive,
My sky where stars have fallen,
My bare branches in the Fall,
My sand where oceans walk,
My grass where cattle sleep,
My hills where beauty first
Went speechless
Without a word to guide it
Through the ways of wonder.
Only you could trace the paths
Of memory in my face.
Only you could touch
The empty space of me
When I am gone.

ELLIS ISLAND

We've all passed through it or should
That place between our mother's thighs
We all arrive at nameless,
That place you thought you were the first
To glimpse,
That Eden and you the only Adam,
Before you even saw
The tree of knowledge
Up ahead
And the sign that said
Trespassers will be persecuted,
Or so you believed for years
Until you figured out
That nice Freudian distinction
Between prosecution
And persecution
And wiped the egg of ignorance
Off your face.
Ah Ellis Island.
It's good to go there again
Once in a while
And put your arms around
The tree of knowledge
Until Jahweh screams at you
For pawing your mother!

FILIPPO LIPPI

They say in Prato
He was paid too much
For making Salome
On stone
Seem like flesh
That any man
Would die for
Except perhaps the Baptist.
Are there really
Any coins
To pay him
For the look in
Herod's eyes
When death unveiled
Slid towards him
On a woman's thigh
And asked him
If he cared to dance?

FREUD 1939

With half a mouth
In his final years,
Wholeheartedly,
Sun and retina
Aligned with tilted
Manuscript,
Lightning and silent
Thunder of thoughts
Flashing within,
Pen on paper
Correcting,
Revising,
Bearing witness
As jack-boots
Clacked
On cobbles
And history
Held words by the throat,
The voice poured
Out of the cracked vessel
Like a prophet's curse:
"Death is not inside you
'til you stare it down,
the dream is only yours
when you awaken."

SUICIDE

Kick chair,
Jump from ceiling,
Neck the rope
That tears
Breath
From bellows of body.
Tomorrow,
Uplifted,
Breathless,
You will have
None of it,
When someone
Cuts you down to size,
Memory
A hang over,
A lost cause,
A rope of broken love
Outside you,
A rope of broken love
Inside you.

FUGUE IN FIVE VOICES

1.
Psychoanalysis

The child you were
You *will* again
To speak for you
As if *his* magic
Sleight of hand
Could trick you
And make illusion
The breast
You wean from once again
As whinnying mouth
With the bit
Of the future in it
Clenches words
That nourish,
Gives appetite
Abiding taste,
Lust its name.

2.
Love

My heart
Red with dreamblood
And red with waking desire
Pours out its song of hunger

FUGUE IN FIVE VOICES

As Time furrows flesh
Without our bidding
And sows the future out of crops
Of dying flesh.

3.
Poem

Part of it
Like dream
A gift unbidden,
The rest
A crafty tongue
Must shape
Into a cobbled thing
Word on word
Like stone on stone
In dry wall
Until
Like rain
Or petal
Or leafgreen
It comes at you
With a startle!

FUGUE IN FIVE VOICES

4.
Origins

We are born
From dreams
We can't remember.
We live in air
We hardly breathe.
We die
Like all great mysteries
Without a proper ending.

5.
Oedipus

Can you believe
What they're saying
About me,
That I mounted her,
Murdered him?
What child
Would dream
Of such a thing,
Unless like sphinx
He knew
The nothing
He crawled out of
And the nothing
Crawling in again
At breathing's end.

FIRENZE

At night the Arno
Is constellation
Not river,
Flowing through sky
Not city.
By day, pinned down again,
Bridges fastening it in place,
It moans like a bound animal.
Why travel ever
To another city:
All the history you can stand
Is packed into these alleys,
These resounding stones
Arnolfo put together
A thousand years ago,
His vision all over you,
Peering down from above
Like the eye of an eagle.
You can still smell the monk's flesh
In the Piazza,
If you lean your nose into history,
Memory like a child in the dark
With eyes closed,
Shutting in what cannot be shut out.

SONNET: CHARON'S TEARS

With Robert Frost I swim across the lake
Reciting poems I mean; "Birches", "Mending
Wall" enough to get across. I take
Theses poems and others without ending
As if lake water under flesh could drop
A man across eternity where Charon leers
O'er Dirce. If her beauty is not sop
Enough, what else to offer but a sop of tears?
In the lake I see an image of the self
With murder in its mouth. Is it the osprey's shade
Above I swim towards, a distant shelf
Of all I am and all that memory made?
I do not swim alone: I swim with Frost,
Blood of poems in water, nothing lost.

GLENN GOULD'S HUMMING

Bach at his fingertips,
Each note
A communion
Well-tempered, uncanny
Between creator
And performer,
The timeless quavers of the dead
Refined again
In the rhythms of the living,
Art patered
Once and for all
In the quirky ideal of his playing,
In the liquid lineage
Of music,
Did he still need
To hum, however,
Sing along
Under his breath,
Like a child
At the breast
Sucking for words
But finding only
The miracle of mouthing,
A strange gruel of meaning
In his throat,
And the first gritty taste
Of the ivory of sound.

ICARUS

Icarus,
Your father was a fool.
He could not see
The legacy
Of your exorbitant flight:
The wax
And feathers
Of your broken wings
Washed up
At Kitty Hawk.

GOLDA (1898-1978)

"The man who doesn't believe in miracles is not a realist."
—David Ben Gurion

She had a pogrom in her head
Called memory.
The nails her father drove
Into boards over the door
To keep the wolf of prejudice
From her home
Landed in her head.
(She was six, in the Ukraine,
Memory hiding
Inside her skull,
Reality beyond her skull
Looking her in the eye
Like snake.)
She would keep one eye
On the snake for ever
Even as she planted
Strawberries in the desert,
Lettuce in the sand.
She whispered
In the desert's frantic ear
Until it slept.
It was only when she died
We learnt of chronic leukemia.
She had run the country,
Death inside her
Like a secret pogrom,

GOLDA (1898-1978)

Her whole body
Steeled against it
Like one of her father's nails,
Determined to keep it out.
Death has won no victory.
Golda lives,
Her memory
A nail of flesh
Driven in the earth,
The rust of her
Ripening the desert.

HOLOCAUST MEMORIAL DAY

At dawn
The dead arose again,
Millions of specters
Brighter than the sun.
By noon
The stench of memory
Was unbearable,
As if all graves
Re-opened,
The dead breathing
Their last again.
By night
The stench of the living
Was unbearable
As if all clothes
Were banished,
And naked crime
Hadn't a stitch
To wear,
And even shame
Went barefoot.
And then the silence.
And then the screams again.
And then the dreams
That would not stop.

JOSEPH OF NAZARETH

He was *your* son no matter
What the gospel says.
Who plucked him from the grass
After a fall beneath the cedars?
Who sang him to sleep with a lilting song?
Whose arms swaddled his night fears?
Whose arms raised him skyward,
And whose arms were there again
When the sky released him? Who felt him
Kicking, months before the waters broke?
Who felt him kicking years later
And took pride in the distance feet had traveled?
Who gave him scraps of wood
From the carpenter's table, his first playthings?
Whose accent did his words climb
Before they found the scaffold of their own voice?
Who put wind in a fretted reed and made
A whistle of music for a child's ears only?
Who put the ocean in a shell?
Who called the stars by their proper names?
Who said the stars had Arabian names
But no nation owned them?
Who said the dark could be afraid
Like children, but only a child could lead it
Through brambled dreams
On its way toward morning?
Who said flesh was born without a name
But would die to defend it?
Who said the sun is never further from you
Than the light of my face above you?

JOSEPH OF NAZARETH

Who bit his tongue to save a virgin's face,
When the whole of Nazareth scoffed
"Annunciation!" Wasn't he the spit and image
Of your human face, and who in his right mind
Has ever seen the face of god?
Wasn't it you he addressed and not a phantom,
When he cried:
"Father forgive them,
For they know not what they do.
Father forgive them
For not recognizing you."

JUDAS IN PARADISE

After the betrayal
After the remorse
After the breakneck rope
After soul slipped noose
And entered heaven
To fly in the face of god
And curse the savior
Fall guy of history
Who crossed
Your palm with silver
For Christ's sake at Calvary
After the betrayal
After the remorse
After the breakneck rope
And thirty pieces of silver
Strewn about your feet
Like petals
Of the doomed flower
Of hope
You once imagined yourself
Did you forgive the gods who used you
Or did you turn on your heel
In Paradise
And hang yourself all over again?

AT DEATH'S DOOR

"There's none of us getting out of this alive"
Jack said, lugging his pail of water.
"If you can get through life, you can get through anything"
Jill countered.
"So let's enjoy the fetching"
Jack said, scratching his broken crown.
"And the tumbling after"
Jill said.

MARCUS AURELIUS

He held the eel
Of meaning
Captive
In his startled hands,
The slither and feel
Of all the twists
And turns
Of its escape
His sole possession
For a moment only,
Until empty handed
Again
All he held
Was memory
Wriggling, dancing
To the tune of loss,
As if loss enacted
Were the thing itself
And not its opposite.
He was five
When the eel
Slipped through the memory
Of his fingers
And now at five and sixty
Could he ever
Be sure

MARCUS AURELIUS

In the lost and found shop
Of the heart,
What it was he held
In the hollow of a hand
Before the letting-go?

ON LEARNING ROBERT FROST'S "BIRCHES" BY HEART

The trees are in me now,
The boy too,
The bent branches,
The girls' hair
Drying in the sun,
The climbing above the brim,
The letting go,
The rush of gravity,
The wild descent,
The sure-footed feel
As the self spills
Out of the pitcher
Of the sky
Into the arms
Of grounded expectation.
The poem is in me now
Like a dream
Learnt by heart
Before the breaking.

NIGHT PRAYER

> "Poetry can only be made
> by looking into that little
> infinite faltering eternal flame
> that one calls the self."
> —W.B. Yeats

Lower me into the dream house.
Dawn can pull me out.
Down there the dead can whisper.
Down there the dead can shout.

"Do you believe in ghosts?"
She asked with a swagger of her head.
"No, madam, I've seen far too many
For myself" was all that Coleridge said.

The moving moon was restless.
The stars were almost spent.
Dawn was a dream on the hillside,
Less real than a tinker's tent.

The child put the dream in his pocket.
Like a ghost, when he loses his way,
In the dazzle and excess of brilliance
It adds some more light to his day.

POETRY

> "The sea grows old in it."
> —Marianne Moore

When it works it's a wonder.
But what does working mean?
You take a little engine of words,
Wind it up, and it runs off
At the mouth, like clock-work?
Not quite!
It's more like dream thoughts:
Restless things that won't be known
Until they change into
Something they are not
The better to know what they are.
But that says nothing. Start again.
"I too dislike it." Moore's the pity!
Like dream, you wake up with it
And then like dream, it's gone,
Only to return whenever a sleeve
Of memory hooks on bramble,
And you're trapped like fish mouth
Until you wriggle free,
Missing the captivity then
That set you loose
From moorings
For a brambled instant
Time wrenched

POETRY

From wrist,
Bell tower,
Civil no more,
A wild timeless piece
Of the sun again
For one eternal moment
Under the ancestral skies
And all the fallen stars.

PASTORALE

Late August
In Romagna.
The fields
Blossomed
With peasants
Wearing colors
That match
The fruit they pick,
Their bent bodies
As much a part
Of the earth,
As the grass
They lean on,
The quiet architecture
Of their labor,
Older than Pomposa.
You can taste
Their sweetness
In the grapes.

ODE TO A NEW YEAR

Come, not because you are new nor that the old
Has worn out its welcome. Come rather as a friend
Who knows to let himself in without being told
And out without imagining it's the end.
All this talk of new and old is Time's
Revenge against the force that splits hairs
And atoms, counts syllables, rhymes
Instead of freeing the furtive word that dares.
I mean Time is only a convention,
A trick mortality came up with to while
Away the doomed hours, an invention
To measure human folly but never smile.
Have you ever seen a wrist watch on the flowers,
Although their days are numbered more than ours?

SEDER

Gather round a table.
Break bread.
Tell the old story,
The truth unleavened,
The bitter and the sweet,
The old story
Of flesh,
The mind
Like a bloom
That knows
The fall of petals,
Knows the scythe
Before the wind
Unsheaths the blade,
Knows the music
The wind makes
Out of falling
Before a note is struck.
Tell how the desert
Wandered
And the sea flowed
Into the veins
Of Bedouin
And prophet,
History an after-taste
Of hunger
In the mouth of man.
Tell how hand-shake
Was born
And bloodshed.

SEDER

Tell how a bridge
Spans
Both sides of a river,
How the earth
Is not divided
By a stream,
But doubly nourished.
Tell how dreams
Invented mirrors
So that sleep
Could see its face
In darkness.
Tell how it recognized
Itself
And didn't
When it woke.
Gather round a table.
Break bread.
Tell the old story,
The truth unleavened,
The bitter and the sweet,
The old story of flesh,
The mind
Like a bloom
That knows
The fall of petals
And rises
To the cadence
Of its song.

SEPTEMBER

"We name the months to make them intimate"
She said
"As if they'd do our bidding called by name."
"Metronomic, cosmic clocks!" he said,
"Do you think they care about a heart's
Hesitance, a grief that can't remember
What it's lost, or never found, the unheard
Music, the rubato, the broken rhythms,
The starts and stops that clear a space for......"
"For what?" she asked.
"For thought, for love's lonely larcenies,
For hate, for second thoughts, for......."
"For what?" she asked again.
"For leaves of flesh" he said, "that cannot stand
The fall, that know no season other than the death
Heart knows when, love fled, blood's
A stranger to itself by the time it hits
The wrist." "You want to be adored" she said.
"I'd settle for love" he said. "That's not settling.
That's the summit for all us earthly climbers."
Silence. Truth, like a weightless weight on him,
Bore him up. "There's gravity in all falling"
"Yes. We name the falling months" she said.
"Call your love September. It will come
When you call, again and again and again
Like memory, like dreaming, like the word for
Spring."

SNOW

Out of your element into another you fall
Weightless, as if gravity had no claim
On you. More intimate than rain you call
To us, who fall from birth to death, the same
As you. Your captive atoms hold the light
As if the sky were breathing through a veil
Of lace, and in the oceans of the night
You drift, a phantom ship with phantom sail.
Unreal, you seem a thing of memory, more
Than life, as if a child at play, or
A dream that never can awaken before
The night reviews in darkness what dreaming's for.
You fall in silence, a ghost without a name,
Content that no two snowflakes are the same.

SONNET FOR ARNIE RICHARDS

If you're eighty now you must have been twenty-six
At Kennedy's Inauguration, when Frost
Read The Gift Outright, his hair in the wind a mix
Of dawn and starlight, the poem itself lost
In cadence for an instant, then found again in rise
And fall, in lilt of voice, in gesture, Time,
Captive in memory, the only pulse we prize,
Or Time eternal trapped in verse or rhyme.
Rebel friend, you made a rampart, an echo
Of your voice to mind and remind all
Who stumble, fall, rise up again, go
On, when going's impossible, to port of call.
Time's not the only gift outright: the heart's
A constant daring and love's a thing apart.

DIALOGUE

(FOR SHELLY BACH)

"The mind's your business?" the child asked. "Yes."
The man said. "All my life it's been."
"Getting inside the blows, can you still bless
The fist when it's your own? What I mean
Is, can a mouth both bite and kiss?"
Then the child fell silent like the hush
That follows after thunder. "It's like this"
The man said: "The wind goes through a bush;
It doesn't break it. Inside the blows
Love and hate settle down. They play
House, the way a thorn, the way a rose
Lives under a single roofing." "I say"
Said the child "inside the blows is love testing
The future, while all the wars of the past are resting?"

SONNET FOR A NEW YEAR

After solstice, after the killing of the wren
Then what? The year revives itself
Calling on the past, the now and then
Of Time tectonic, ageless ocean's shelf
On the go underneath the all
Of it as continents drift and stones under-
Foot shift a little as thoughts call
Out to other thoughts and pull asunder
Certainties. This is the soil we walk
On, always have. Gravity bends more
Than light, speech itself, its very talk
And wavelength as bent as the wrinkled shore.
There is a sea within us, our spectred schemes
Doom driven, salt in the wound of dreams.

SWEENEY ASTRAY

In a country of madmen
They called me mad,
As if distinction mattered
In that ant-heap?
"Claim a dog has rabies
And you can throw stones at him."
I was a rabid cur
In the bias of their eyes,
I, who could have died
In battle at Moira,
A warrior,
If the bishop hadn't turned on me.
Better dogs after you
Than that holy hound chase
I tell you.
So I took to my tree
And drank milk out of cow-dung
And they called me mad.
But in the pitch of night
When the stars hang low
Like night fruit
I talk to the holy silence
And in all these years
There's been nothing but respect between us:
As night is my witness
I swear, in all these years
It never once talked back to me.

THE GRAVITY OF LOVE

Imagine the future ever falling, never
Feeling its own weight. Einstein saw
It falling, the weightless gravity of it. Whenever
Love falls, the human heart, a law
Unto itself, accelerates beyond
The speed of time, as two hands hold
The future suspended, the way in a pond
The timeless moon ages but never grows old,
As night falls weightless, and dawn
Picks up where stars left off. Love's its own
Science, each human heart drawn
Towards the magnet of another, never again alone.
It is the speed of love each heart must measure,
A kind of weightless falling, a gravity to treasure.

TITHONUS' LAMENT

It was cruel of her to grant me one without the other
Eternal life without eternal youth, so now my skin
Flaps and clatters like a rattling blind in a window while
She awakens in the east aflame, her skin on fire
With beauty unconsumed, mine on fire, burnt to a crisp
Brittle dried up kindling, almost aflame before the flint
Is struck. No end in sight either, my fate merely another
Name for mockery. While poets write about me and curse
Their luck for being mortal, I'll curse the day I glimpsed
    Aurora
Chasing the last stars away, night at her feet bedazzled
In flight from such resplendent beauty, her nakedness falling
From her like an invisible veil. Ah my heart still leaps
In its old cage like a frantic songbird, can only sing in such
Captivity, the chains of love I mean, her lips on mine
In the old days when love was moist, lip on lip, no word
Between us ever, speech unnecessary, silence chanting
All the tones of love. Even now, memory of such days
Is all I need to perk me up when mirrors refuse to take
Me in, as if it were not my eyes lit their candles, blind
Inanimate sand-borns without my reflection of sunlight
In them. Aurora, break this fated spell and let me die
Young, a robust, burnt out lover in your immortal arms.

A PAINTED GUINEA PIG

"Who painted him?"
A child asked,
When "Guinny" died
And another pet replaced him.
Others took up the cry:
They could not hold
His absence
In their startled hands
So they "painted" him,
Death banished from the nursery
In an instant
With a coat of pigment.
They played a game with Death:
It tricked them;
They tricked it back,
The painted god reviled,
Pinched, starved,
His altar lined with lost lettuce,
His skin pinched,
Bruises concealed
Beneath rumpled fur,
As they abused an upstart
Who dared to leave
And come back cosmetic in costume.
Love did bloom again
Eventual
In the nurseries of Time,
Hate-petalled,
Love-stemmed,
Memory-fed,

A PAINTED GUINEA PIG

As children added grief
To their curriculum,
Singing
"Ashes, ashes"
As petals all fall down,
Even the doomed blossoms of children.

"TOUCH ME. REMIND ME WHO I AM"

In the morning
With eyes closed,
My hand in yours
Like a blind man
It is the feel of holding
That I know
Not the hand itself.
Is that how love
Got started
In the first
Out of womb
Place
When touch
Hurled flesh
Out of itself
Into the unknown
Strange familiarity
Of desire?

WINDMILL'S SONG

I catch the scruff of the wind
And circles run;
Split seeds of wheat
Release the sun.
What can I show
For all my turning?
Human bread
And human yearning.

VINCENT'S SONG

I pulled a leaf
From Autumn's face
And carried it
Shivering in cupped palms
To my secret lover.
She was a summer girl
Saw nothing in a leaf,
Saw nothing in the Fall
But falling
And let the matter drop.
I pulled a star
From the face of night
And carried quicksilver
In cupped palms to her.
She tasted nothing
Of its liquid light.
She never heard a star
Scream In Prussian blue
Or yellow ochre.
She never saw night hiding
In the shame of dawn.
I pulled a dream
From the marrow
Of my heart for her,
Mounted it on canvas:
Through it the night itself
Could speak, find voice
For sorrow's shyness,
The courage only fear can mirror:

VINCENT'S SONG

But the syllables fell like seed
On granite.
It was then I cut her ear
To spite her face,
Not knowing
In the looking-glass of fear
My weeping face was hers,
Her bleeding face was mine.

PRAGUE

In the synagogue
A Stonehenge
Of headstones,
The dead in disarray,
The crooked timber
Of humanity
Topsy-turvy
In the theater
Of death
As in life
As Kant warned,
Time and weather
And groundswell
Uprooting a symmetry
Once planned by shovel,
As the burial society
Took the medieval
Measure of the earth
Doing their level best,
Centuries,
Like cold-eyed
Horsemen,
Pass and weep
As night whispers
Kol Nidrah
In stone ears
On the Charles Bridge,
The crowds like dust
In frantic motion,

PRAGUE

Grief
No marionette
Behind the curtain
Of the heart.

THE PAST

As dawn was tearing loose from darkness
We heard the screeching.
"A blue jay" I said.
"A dog " you said.
"That dog has wings" I said.
"Maybe it's a crow" you said.
"Maitre corbeau tenait dans son bec un fromage.
Maitre Renard par l'odeur alleche tentait a peu pres
    ce langage.
That's a war memory" you said.
"Bologna 1942.
I was eager to go to school.
I couldn't.
I learnt French instead from a tutor.
We were Jews my father said,
And I should be silent.
I learnt French and fear and silence
That year.
In no time.
I was six.
I understood everything.
I understood nothing.
We went hiding in the woods.
Three women.
Mother, grandmother, child.
The trees held up the sky
Except when the sky fell
Splintered,
Through all the cracks and spaces
Between the branches.

THE PAST

We heard a lot of screeching in the night.
We heard it in daylight too.
We heard the earth scraping
Against the sky.
We heard blood screaming to get out.
We heard bells and bullets and bombs.
We walked on tightropes
Over mined roadways,
Donkeys first."
As dawn was tearing loose from darkness
We heard the screeching again.
"A blue jay" I said.
"A dog" you said.
"It's the past." I said.
"Yes, it's the past." you said.

RESOLUTIONS

I shall take a new blade to my beard and see
If I can make it last until eternity.
I shall squeeze the truth out of memory even if it kills me.
I shall never confuse history and truth:
The history of slaves written by masters is obscenity.
I shall measure my words, attach them to the surface
Of reality and see how far I can make them go: if
There are words left over I shall make poems out of them.
I shall use magic sparingly, except when I'm in love,
A contradiction I will cherish.
I will build a better net for catching dreams with:
I will learn to speak their foreign language.
I will learn to walk out of my dreams at night
the way Tibetans do
and explore the mysteries of science.
I will kill god again and again and not the impostors
he keeps fooling us with.
I will predict the past so that the future need not be foretold,
And live in the ever-present full of memory and desire.
I will ask the seasons to teach me how to age,
And "go off and bear me like the Time" whatever
Shakespeare meant by that.
I will walk in circles on a flat world until
I get the hang of space-time and learn to bend
Light with the weightless gravity of thinking.
I will bring love and hate together:
They grew up in the same cradle.
The only crime is boredom: I shall expose it.

RESOLUTIONS

My lens shall always be the eyes of children:
They never age because they never
take the light for granted.
Resolutions are like fish or houseguests:
After three days they stink: I will make no more.

PUTTING IN THE SPRING

Each April
Beside perennial crocus
Daffodil and snowdrop
With a conceit of flesh
That dares to upstage
Nature,
Armed with pansies
I prepare their graves
In window box and rockery
And cradle them snug.
It's not the sticks of winter
I imagine
That herds these seeds
Through the darkness
Of the final season
But a memory of spring,
A grain of instinct
Buried in the seed
Now unburied
In a burst of bloom.
If robins
In their bones
Know a rain song
From a sun song.
Is it only a conceit of flesh,
Its skeletal future
In doomed bones,
Its protest
Against the insolence
Of death,

PUTTING IN THE SPRING

That green thumbs
The fragile
Mortality of
Pansies in the earth
Each April
As it's putting in the spring?

TO A CHILD AT THE END OF ANALYSIS

"Flowers grow so fast"
He said
"Children take a while"
All of the time he knew
So far,
All seven years of it
Compressed inside the wish
To grow as fast
As daffodils
And a swallow's daring.
Flowers and flesh
All one to him
In the poetry of his mind.
He left.
His mother kissed his forehead
And waved back
At an analyst
Whose wings had tipped
An eagle's wings
Before they learnt to fly.

www.ingramcontent.com/pod-product-compliance
Lightning Source LLC
Chambersburg PA
CBHW070632300426
44113CB00010B/1749